MY HERO SEARCH

Author
Antoinette P. Balfour

Illustrations By
Antoinette P. Balfour
Ka'Tiya A. Bloomfield

MY HERO SEARCH

Illustrations By
Antoinette P. Balfour
Ka'Tiya A. Bloomfield

ISBN: 978-1-7373034-1-1

Library of Congress Control Number: 2024905253

DEDICATION AND HONOR

This book is dedicated to my great-granddaughter Nala. It is my hope that she will grow to understand the importance of using the leadership qualities that she has to be the best that she can be, which includes being her own hero.

Additionally, to my granddaughters Ka'Myia and Ka'Tiya, I honor you and hope you understand that most importantly is what you think of yourselves and not what others think of you. It is my desire that you comprehend that the hero in you is only a mindset away. It is up to you to stand strong and affirm your might as your own hero.

Finally I would like to pay tribute to Ka'Tiya whose two illustrations below I used in this book. She created them as a young child and left them behind as she moved on with her life. Thanks Ka'Tiya.

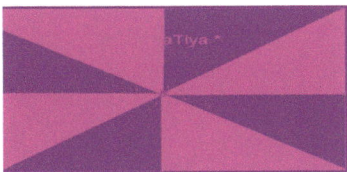

My Hero.

Where oh where

is that special one?

Somewhere on earth

beneath the

bright shinnny sun.

But

where

?

On the search

for my hero,

I searched up high.

I kept going

and going,

Then I searched

Down Below.

I searched from house to house and from door to door.

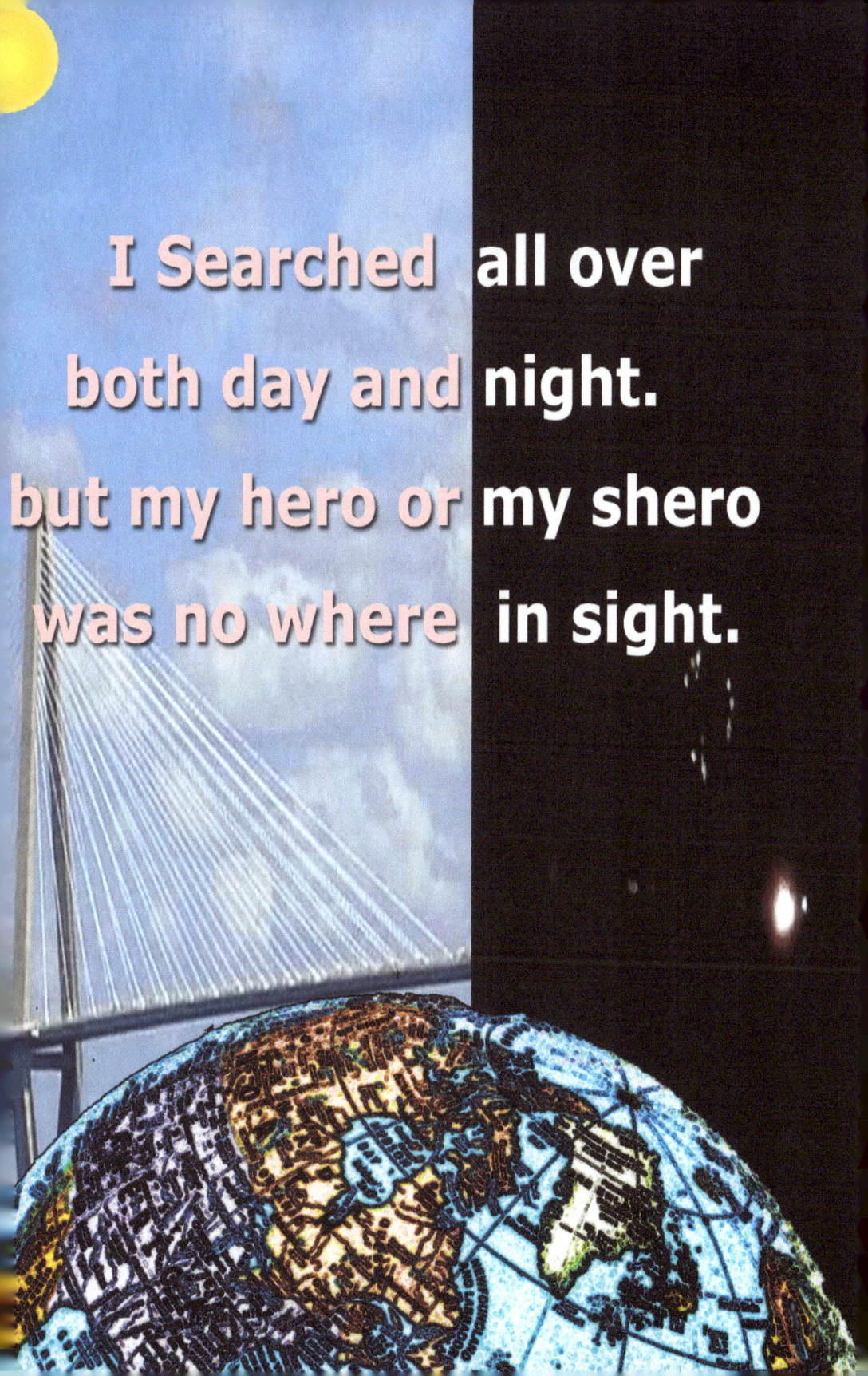

I Searched all over
both day and night.
but my hero or my shero
was no where in sight.

I

asked myself

what a

hero should be?

When I find my hero or my shero, what should I see?

When I find my hero,

what my hero

should do:

Is be someone

who can always

be true.

Who will do

the right thing,

No matter what

others do.

Do The

Right Thing

Award

My hero is

far from perfect,

But like no other

you will find:

With its' own flaws

and challenges,

my hero is one of a kind.

Not Perfect

Temperment

Learning Style

Interests

Hobbies

Social Dynamics

Family Structure

My hero

looks out for me

and encourages me

to lead my own team.

Finding my hero

was not easy for me.

I was not looking

in the places

that my hero

would be.

When there was

no where else to look

and no where else to go,

I asked myself again,

"Where is my hero?"

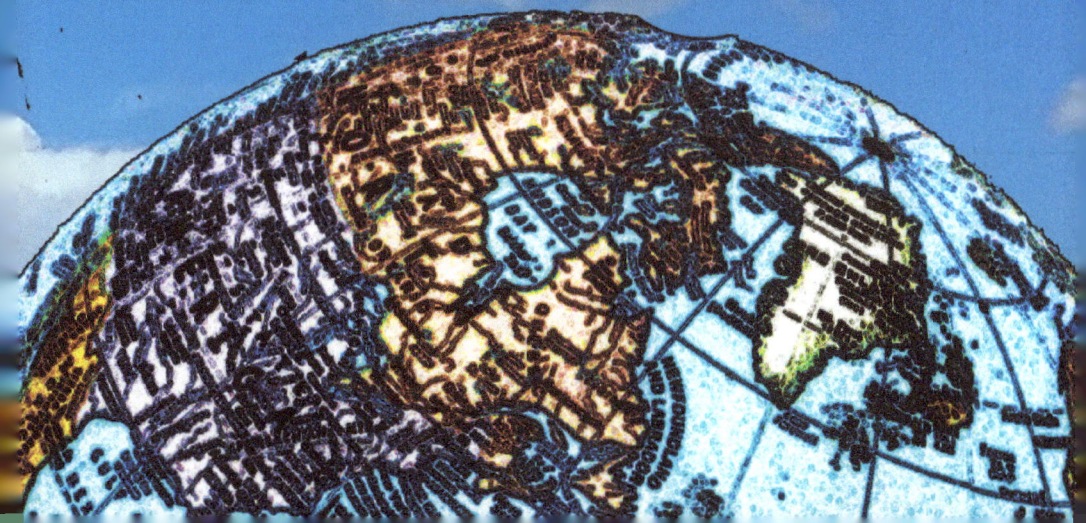

Then I looked

into the mirror and

I began to see,

a reflection of

all of the qualities

that in my hero should be.

Always

be
your

own

hero.

Paste your picture below.

Your Name

DISCUSSION PROMPT

Does a hero have to be perfect?

What are some examples of how heroes choose their own path or make their own choices?

Do heroes look and act like everyone else?

Why do you think heroes make different choices than others?

What do heroes have that others don't have?

Who is your favorite hero?

What hero qualities do you see in yourself?

www.ingramcontent.com/pod-product-compliance
Lightning Source LLC
Chambersburg PA
CBHW041442290326
41933CB00034B/29